INSPIRATIONAL
QUOTES TO LIVE
BY

Dr. Earl Bracy, Clinical Psychologist

PROMINENT
BOOKS

5830 E 2nd St, Ste 7000 #9983
Casper, WY 82609
USA

May these quotes uplift all of the clients that I have worked with. They have taught me as much as I have taught them.

LIFE ABSENT OF LOVE IS
LIKE A BARREN LAND.

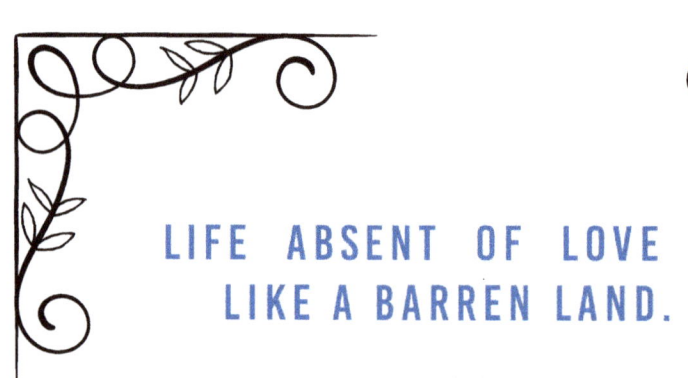

GIVING TO OTHERS IS LIKE A BOOMERANG.   IT   COMES BACK TO YOU.

3

IF YOU CANNOT CHANGE THE
WORLD, CHANGE WHAT IS IN
YOUR LITTLE CORNER OF THE
WORLD.

IF AT FIRST YOU DON'T SUCCEED,
PERSEVERE   AND   OVERCOME
UNTIL YOU BECOME.

THERE IS NO SUCH WORD AS
GLOOMY. FACE THE WORLD
WITH ENTHUSIASM.

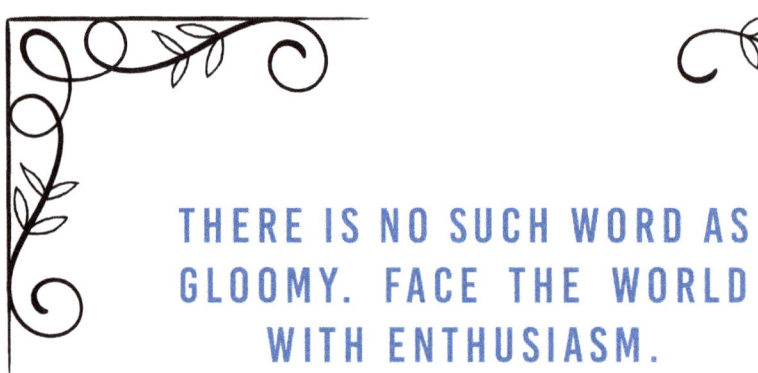

WHENEVER YOU WANT TO
GIVE UP, KEEP YOUR EYES
ON THE LIGHT AT THE END
OF THE TUNNEL.

MOST PEOPLE DO NOT LIKE MONDAY MORNING BUT I SAY, THE WEEK HAS TO START SOMEWHERE.

JUNE   **2022**

M	T	W	T	F	S	S
	1	2	3	4	5	6
7	8	9	10	11	12	13
14	15	16	17	18	19	20
21	22	23	24	25	26	27
28	29	30				

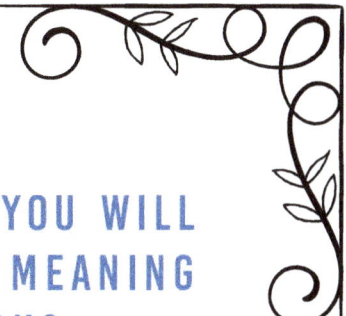

SMILE MORE AND YOU WILL UNDERSTAND THE MEANING OF CONTAGIOUS.

DO NOT BELITTLE ANYONE
BECAUSE THE PERSON YOU
BELITTLE MAY ENTER YOUR
LIFE IN UNFORESEEN WAYS.

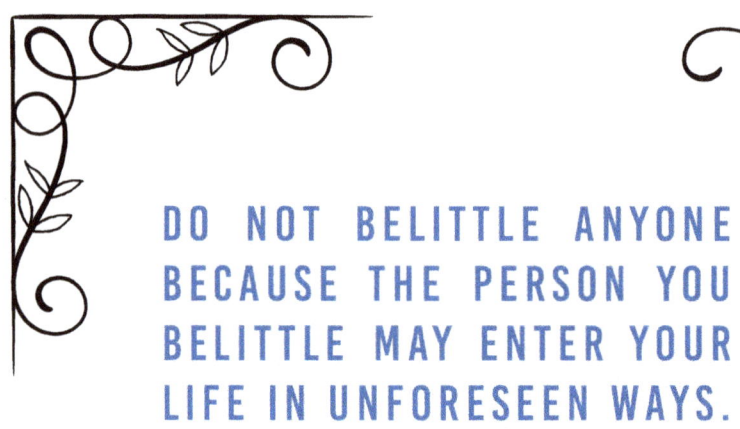

MANY OLDER PEOPLE WILL
OFTEN SAY THAT THEY HAVE
MORE TIME BEHIND THEM
THAN AHEAD OF THEM. I SAY
THAT YOU HAVE MORE TIME
AHEAD OF YOU IF YOU BELIEVE
IN ETERNITY.

WHEN YOU FEEL LIKE
OTHERS ARE PULLING YOU
INTO NEGATIVITY, DARE TO
BE DIFFERENT.

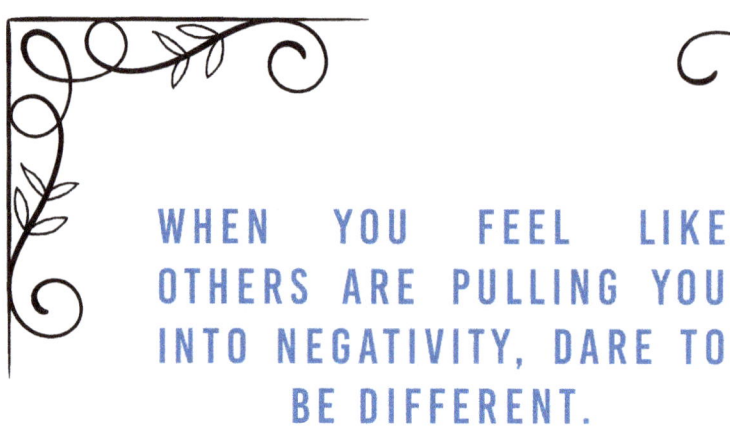

IF YOU FAIL, LEARN FROM YOUR DISAPPOINTMENT AND TEACH OTHERS YOUR SECRET TO SUCCESS.

GOD GAVE US THE GIFT OF
LIFE AND HE SAID TO LOVE
ONE ANOTHER, NOT TO HATE
ONE ANOTHER.

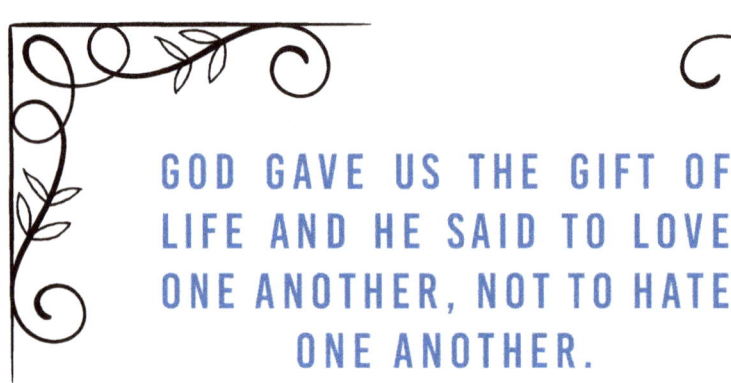

A GIVING HEART IS A HAPPY HEART.

IF AT FIRST YOU DON'T SUCCEED,
KNOW THAT THERE ARE MANY
ROADS TO SUCCESS.

IF YOU WERE IN A ROOM WITH A ROOM FULL OF FAMILIAR PEOPLE AND YOUR EYES WERE CLOSED AND EACH ONE LAUGHED INDIVIDUALLY, YOU WOULD RECOGNIZE EACH ONE'S LAUGH BECAUSE WE ARE ALL DIFFERENT AND UNIQUE.

IF YOUR DREAMS DO NOT
COME TRUE, MAYBE IT IS
BECAUSE YOU DO NOT BE-
LIEVE.

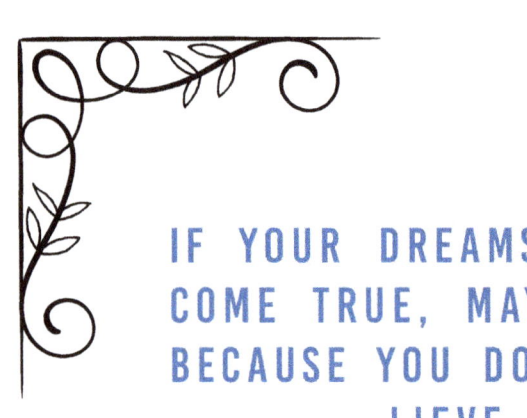

IF YOU TALK INCESSANTLY,
MORE THAN LIKELY YOU ARE
NOT LISTENING.

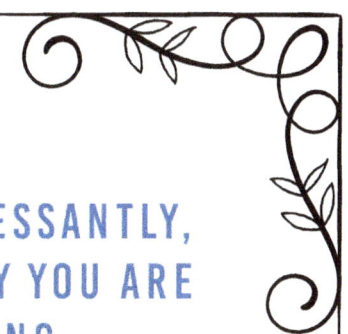

EDUCATION IS THE KEY TO
SUCCESS. USE YOUR KEY TO
UNLOCK THE PATHWAY TO
LEARNING..

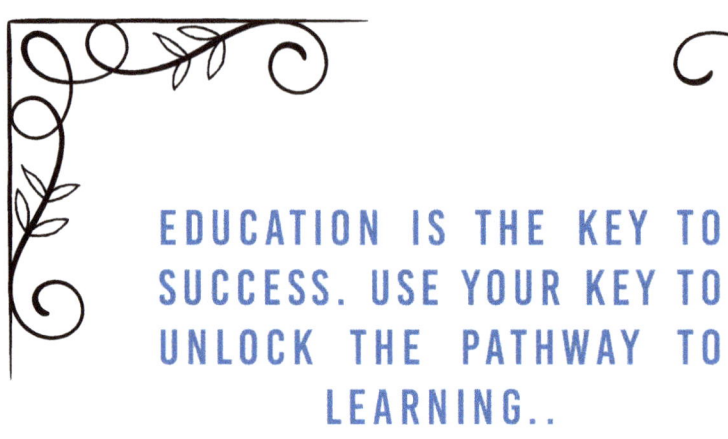

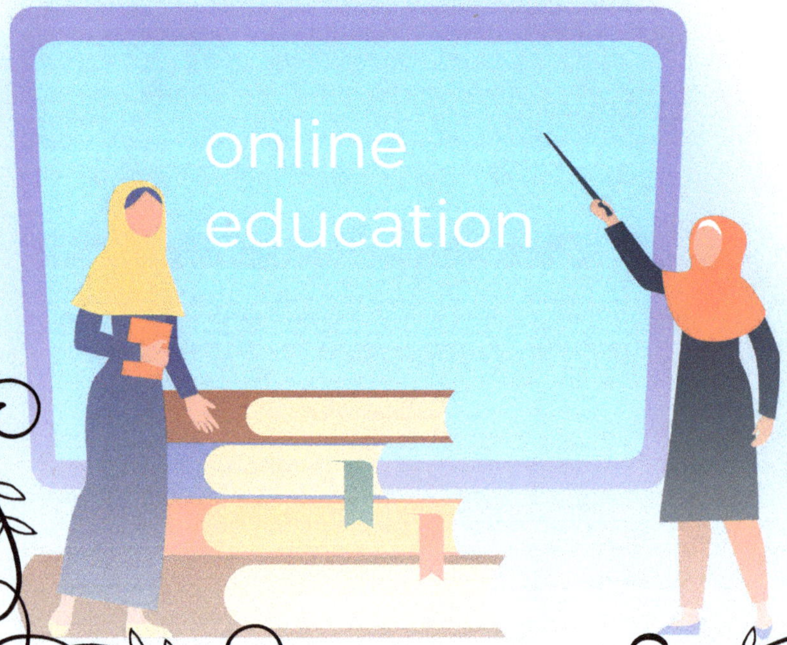

ENJOY ALL TYPES OF WEATHER, WHETHER IT'S RAINY, CLOUDY, SNOWY, FOGGY, WINDY, OR SUNNY. IT'S ALL A GIFT FROM GOD.

YOUR DREAMS WILL NOT
COME TRUE UNLESS YOU
INVEST IN THE EFFORT TO
CHASE THEM.

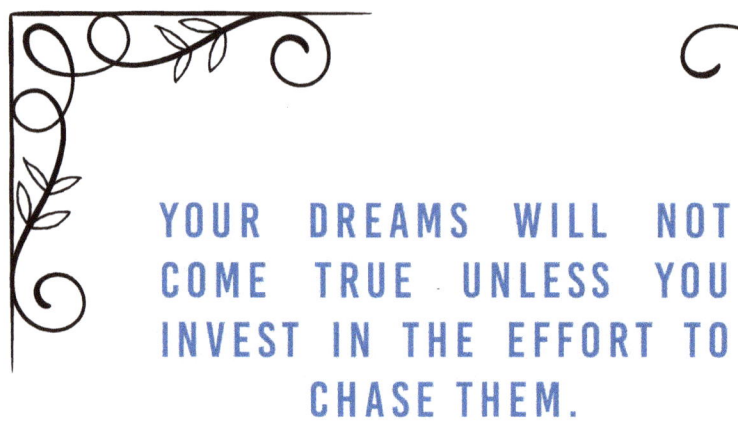

DO NOT SEE OBSTACLE AS
SETBACKS, INSTEAD, SEE
THEM AS OPPORTUNITIES.

ALWAYS DO YOUR PART AND
MORE AND DO NOT WAIT
FOR OTHERS TO STEP UP.

DO NOT BE AFRAID TO FAIL.
IF YOU DO NOT FAIL, YOU DO
NOT LEARN.

IF SOMEONE DISLIKES YOU BECAUSE OF YOUR COLOR OR BACKGROUND, IT IS NOT YOUR PROBLEM BUT THEIRS.

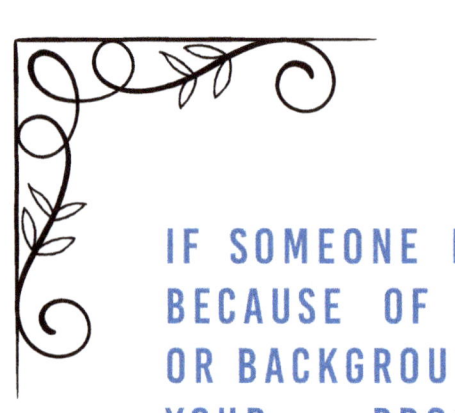

WE ARE WHAT WE DO AND
THINK ALL DAY LONG. BE
THE BEST IN WHAT YOU DO.

CHANGE IS CONSTANT AND
CANNOT BE UNCHANGED.

BE AWARE OF NEGATIVE
PEOPLE. THEY WILL NOT
BOOST YOU BUT WILL
REDUCE YOU.

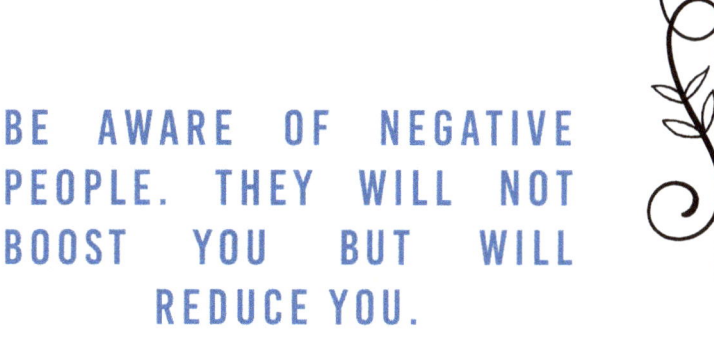

HATE IS LIKE DRIVING IN THE POURING RAIN WITHOUT WIPERS. YOUR SIGHT IS BLINDED.

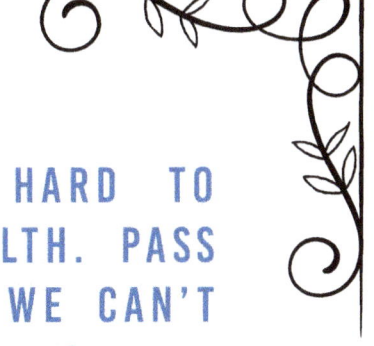

WE WORK SO HARD TO
GATHER UP WEALTH. PASS
IT ON BECAUSE WE CAN'T
TAKE IT WITH US..

COMMUNICATION IS A TWO WAY STREET. MEET THE OTHER PERSON HALFWAY.

WHEN YOU CAN'T CHANGE
THE DIRECTION THINGS ARE
GOING IN YOUR LIFE, TAKE
A DEEP BREATH AND TRY
CONFORMING.

IF YOU WANT IT, GO AFTER IT.

YOU ONLY LIVE ONCE IN
THIS LIFE BUT KNOW THAT
THERE IS AN AFTERLIFE.

BE PATIENT AND AT THE
RIGHT TIME, THE SKY WILL
OPEN UP FOR YOU.

A JEALOUS PERSON IS A DANGEROUS PERSON. BEWARE OF FALSE FRIENDS.

IF OTHER PEOPLE LIE ABOUT YOU, KEEP YOUR COMPOSURE BECAUSE THE TRUTH ALWAYS SHINES THROUGH.

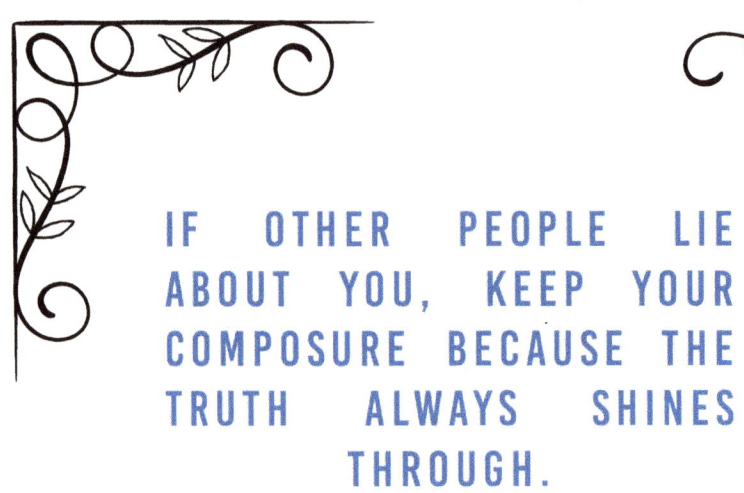

DOGS, CATS, CHILDREN AND BABIES RESPOND TO YOU KINDLY BECAUSE THEY RECOGNIZE A KIND SPIRIT.

SOME PEOPLE SAY LIFE IS A
BITCH AND THEN YOU DIE. I
SAY LIFE IS WHAT YOU MAKE
IT UNTIL YOU DIE.

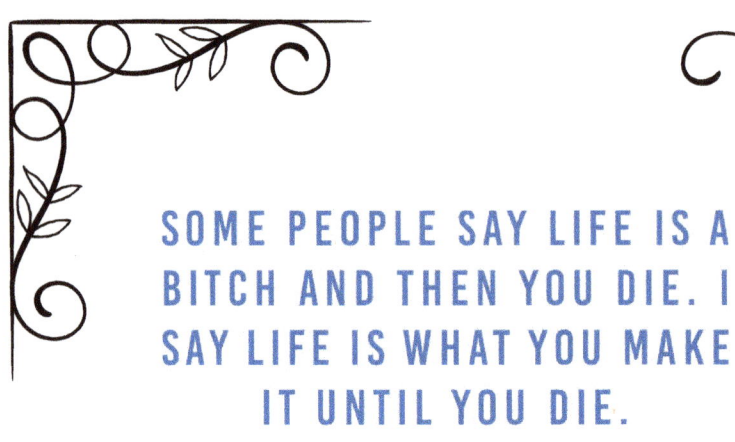

IF YOUR PARENTS AND GRAND-PARENTS FELT UNSUCCESSFUL BECAUSE OF THEIR LIMITED EDUCATION, THEY WERE SUCCESSFUL BECAUSE THEY ARE THE REASON THAT YOU ARE SUCCESSFUL.

YOUR ADULT CHILDREN WILL REMIND YOU OF WHAT YOU DID WRONG IN THEIR CHILDHOOD. ALWAYS DO WHAT IS RIGHT.

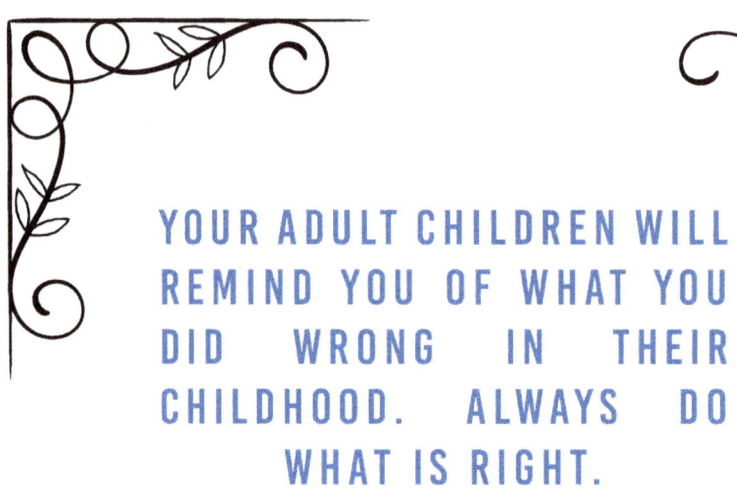

WHEN YOU ARE FLYING IN THE CLOUDS AND YOU EXPERIENCE TURBULENCE AND A LOSS OF VISIBILITY, EVENTUALLY, YOU WILL RISE ABOVE THE CLOUDS AND THERE ARE BLUE SKIES AND SUNSHINE.

WHEN LIFE THROWS YOU A
CURVE BALL, DON'T STEP
OUT OF THE BATTERS BOX,
STAY THE COURSE.

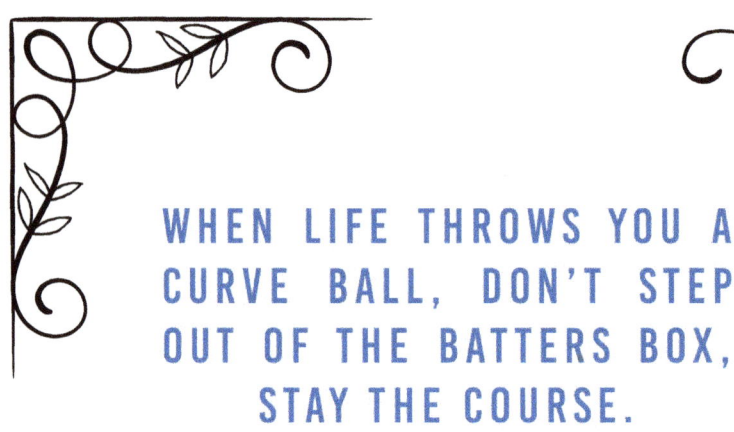

MONDAY IS BLUE MONDAY,
ONLY IF YOU ALLOW IT TO
BE BLUE.

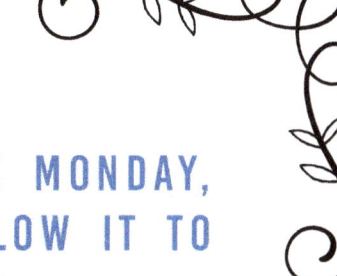

WHEN YOU DO SOMETHING FOR ANOTHER PERSON, DO IT OUT OF SINCERITY AND OUT OF THE GOODNESS OF YOUR HEART, NOT BECAUSE YOU EXPECT SOMETHING IN RETURN.

IF YOU WITNESS SOMEONE
BEING RIDICULED, DISRE-
SPECTED ON DEMEANED
AND YOU SAY NOTHING,
THEN YOU ARE COMPLICIT.
SPEAK UP AND STAND UP.

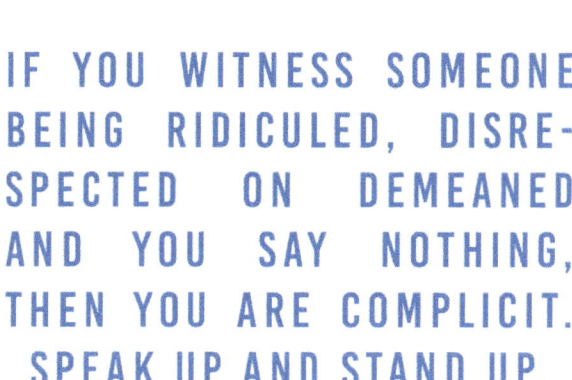

ALWAYS STRIVE FOR EXCEL-LENCE IN ALL THAT YOU DO.

YOU DON'T HAVE TO BE A
FAST RUNNER, JUST PERSE-
VERE AND STICK TO IT AND
SUCCESS IS YOURS.

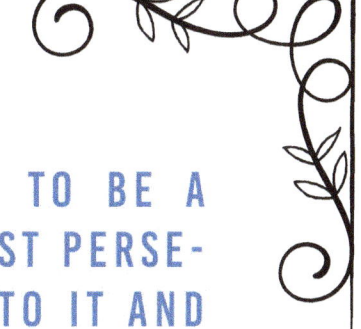

DO NOT LET OTHER PEOPLE'S NEGATIVITY IMPEDE YOUR PROGRESS.

EVERY PERSON WHO HAS TAUGHT US BECOMES PART OF US AND WE BECOME PART OF THEM.

GRANDPARENTS CAN LEARN FROM THEIR GRANDCHILDREN AND GRANDCHILDREN CAN LEARN FROM THEIR GRAND-PARENTS, WHAT IT TAKES TO NAVIGATE THE WORLD SUCCESSFULLY.

ANGER IS THE TORNADO THAT DISRUPTS THE CIR-CUITRY OF THE MIND.

NATURAL ABILITIES SHOULD BE UTILIZED, SHARED AND NOT WASTED.

ACCEPT EACH PERSON AS
THEY ARE. INDIVIDUALISM
IS A GIFT FROM GOD.

WHEN YOU HAVE DIFFICULTY ACCEPTING YOUR OWN MORTALITY, JUST KNOW THAT NO ONE CAME HERE TO STAY.

BE CAREFUL WHAT YOUR THOUGHTS ARE, THEY VERY WELL MAY COME TO FRUITION.

WHEN YOU REACH THE PIN-NACLE OF SUCCESS, DO NOT SNUB THE PEOPLE WHO HELPED YOU GET THERE.

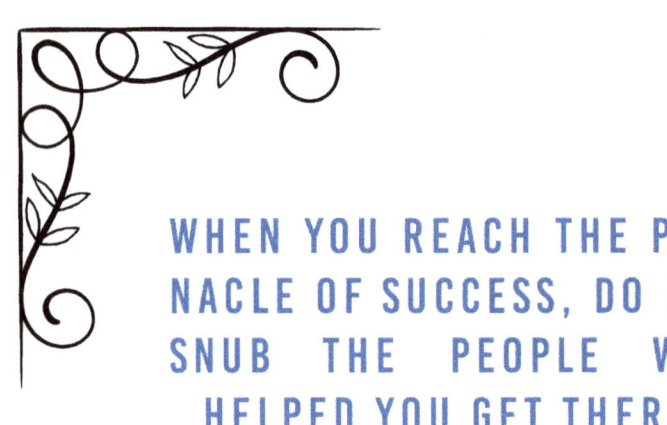

DO NOT LOOK DOWN ON THE POOR BECAUSE OF YOUR WEALTH. THE POOR MAY BE RICHER THAN YOU BECAUSE OF THEIR FAITH AND HUMILITY.

MANY PEOPLE DO NOT LIKE CHANGE BUT EMBRACE CHANGE AND YOU BECOME A CHANGED PERSON.

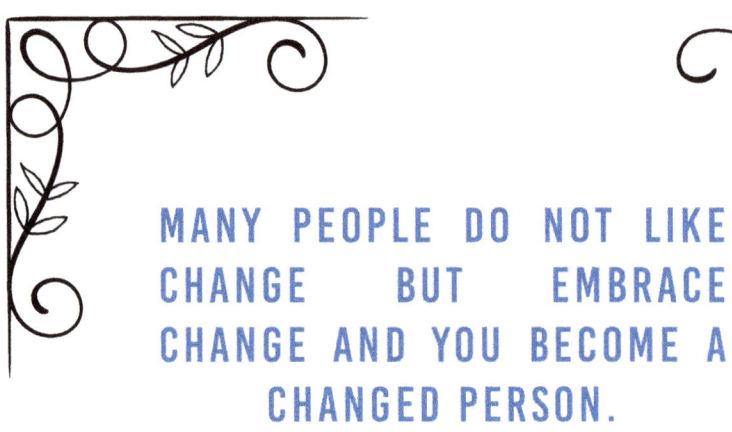

ALWAYS BE BIG ENOUGH AND
ACCEPT FAULT AND TAKE RE-
SPONSIBILITY WHEN YOU ARE
WRONG.

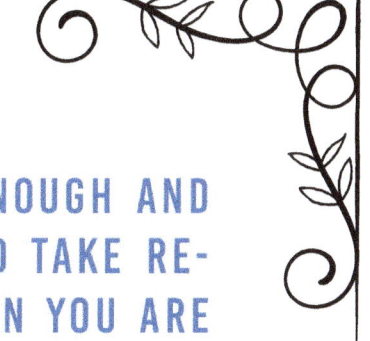

A DRUNK PERSON AND AN ANGRY PERSON HAVE THE SAME THING IN COMMON. THEY CAN EASILY BLACKOUT.

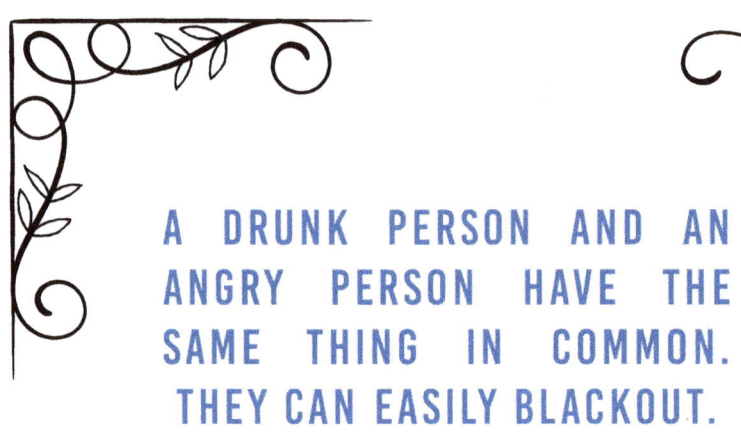

THAT SPECIAL PERSON WILL
NOT COME INTO YOUR LIFE, AS
LONG AS YOU ARE HOLDING ON
TO YOUR PAST.

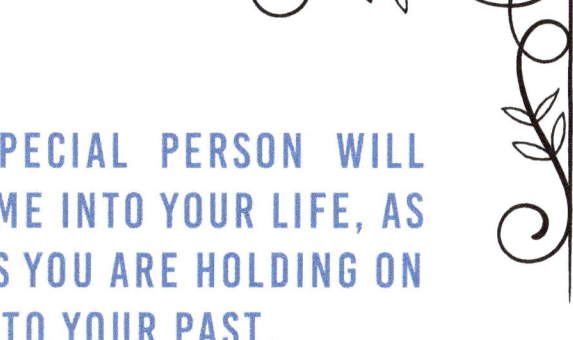

IF YOU ENCOUNTER A PROBLEM, TRY GOING AROUND IT. IF THAT DOESN'T WORK, GO UNDER IT AND IF THAT DOESN'T WORK GO OVER IT. WHEN EVERYTHING FAILS, GO RIGHT THROUGH IT STANDING UPRIGHT WITH CONFIDENCE.

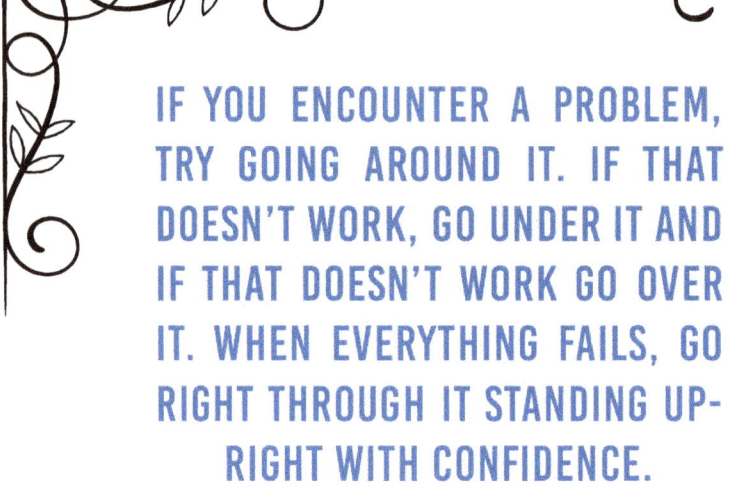

IN FOUR WORDS, I CAN SUM
UP EVERYTHING LIFE HAS
TAUGHT ME. NEVER, NEVER,
GIVE UP.

HUMAN BEINGS ARE LIKE
SNAKES. WE HAVE TO SHED
IN ORDER TO GROW.

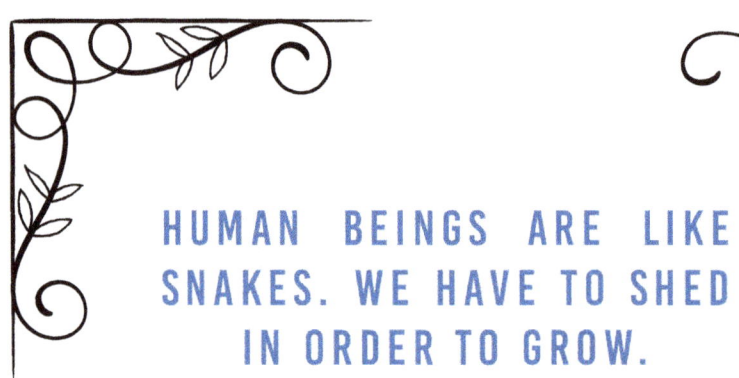

GROWTH TAKES PLACE IN A STIMULATING ENVIRONMENT.

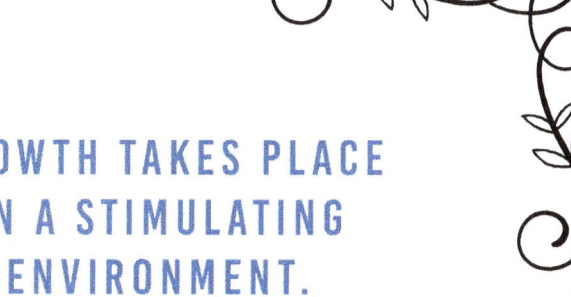

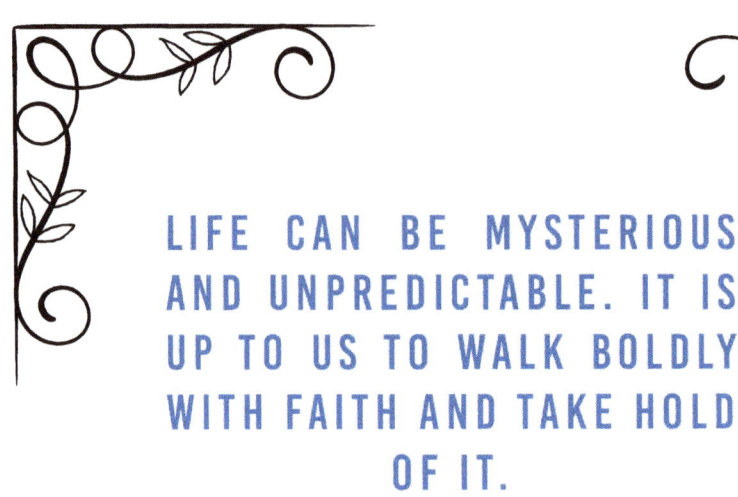

LIFE CAN BE MYSTERIOUS AND UNPREDICTABLE. IT IS UP TO US TO WALK BOLDLY WITH FAITH AND TAKE HOLD OF IT.

REGARDLESS OF WHAT AGE
YOU ARE, ALWAYS STAY IN
MOTION.

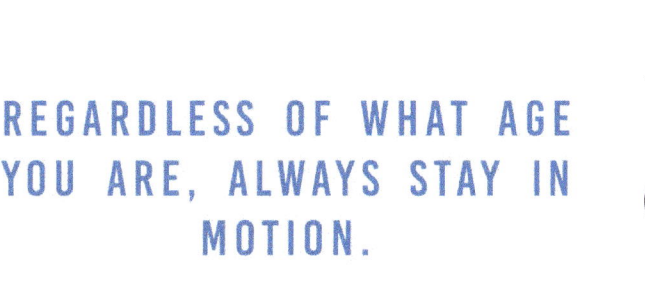

NOT ONLY SHOULD YOU
EXERCISE THE BODY TO
STAY FIT BUT EXERCISE AND
STIMULATE THE MIND FOR
TOTAL FITNESS.

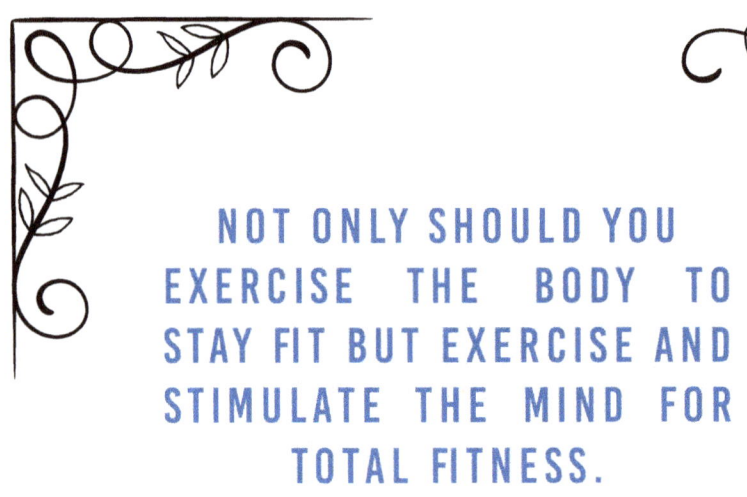

WHEN PEOPLE GREET YOU, THEY USUALLY ASK YOU HOW YOU'RE DOING. WHEN YOU BECOME A SENIOR CITIZEN, THEY ASK YOU HOW ARE YOU FEELING.

YOU MAY HAVE TO GO THROUGH STORMS IN ORDER TO APPRECIATE SUNNY DAYS.

THINGS IN LIFE HAPPEN
WHEN THEY'RE SUPPOSE
TO, NOT ALWAYS WHEN YOU
WANT THEM TO.

WHEN YOU ARE 60, YOUR BODY CAN LOOK THE SAME WAY IT LOOKED AT 30 IF YOU WORK AT IT.

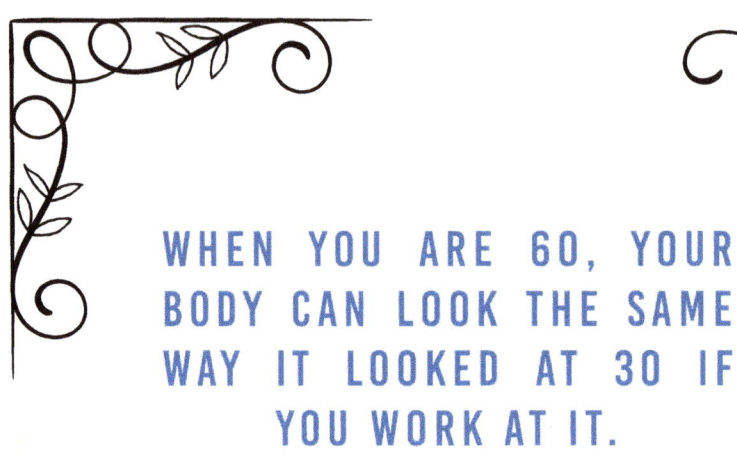

WHEN YOU ARE GRIEVING, PEOPLE ARE GOING TO TELL YOU TO BE STRONG. GRIEVE AT YOUR OWN PACE AND FEEL THE PAIN THAT YOU FEEL.

WHEN OTHERS DOUBT YOU,
KEEP YOUR FOCUS AND STAY
THE COURSE.

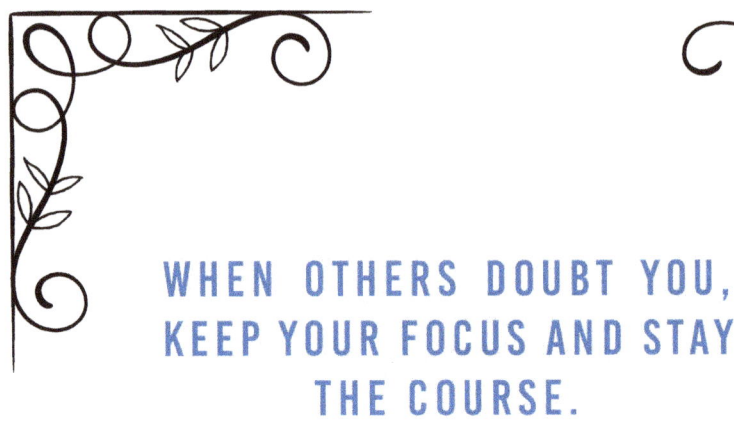

IF ONE SPOUSE IS PRO EDU-
CATION AND THE OTHER IS
NOT, YOUR CHILDREN WILL
BE CONFLICTED AND MAY
NOT VALUE EDUCATION.

WHENEVER YOU HELP THE
LESS FORTUNATE AND DO
NOT EXPECT ANYTHING IN
RETURN, YOUR RETURN
WILL BE TENFOLD.

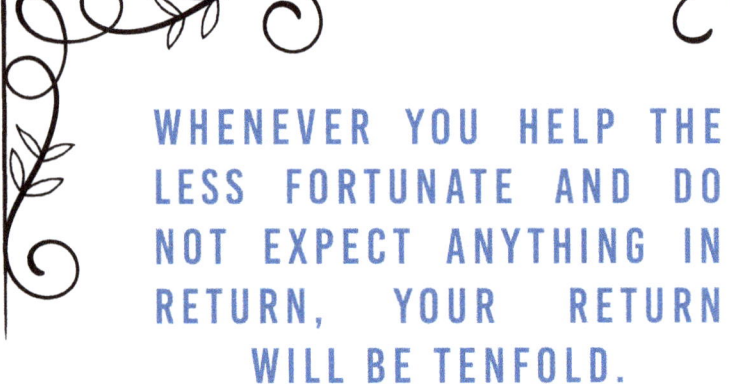

DEATH IS INESCAPABLE.
THEREFORE, LIVE YOUR
BEST LIFE AND LIVE EACH
DAY TO THE FULLEST.

YOU ARE DESTINED TO DIE
BUT YOUR NAME WILL LIVE
ON.

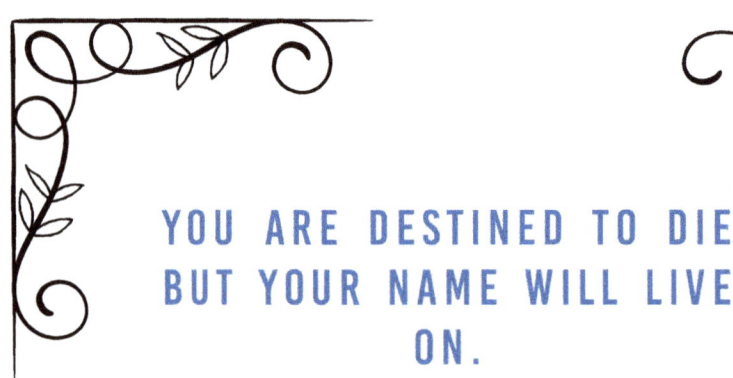

GOOD FRIENDS ARE LIKE FEELING YOUR WAY THROUGH THE DARKNESS. THEY ARE NOT ALWAYS VISIBLE BUT YOU CAN BE ASSURED THAT THEY ARE ALWAYS THERE.

WHEN YOUR HEART IS COLD
AND CALLOUS YOUR MIND
WILL FOLLOW.

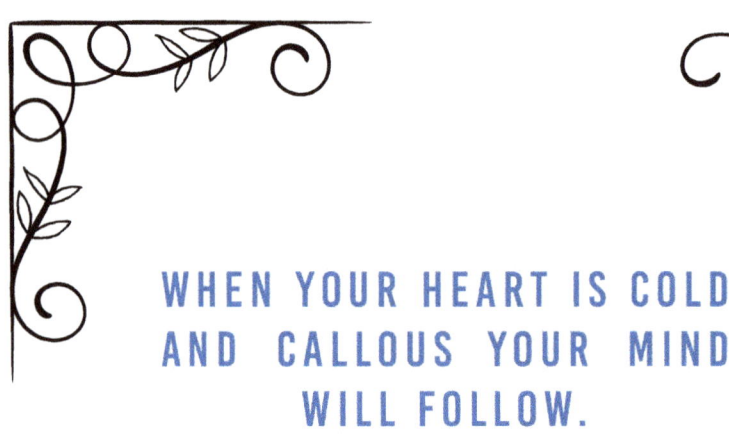

SPREAD YOUR GENEROSITY
BY BEING A GIVER AND NOT
A TAKER.

THE PEOPLE WHO HAVE TAUGHT YOU, WILL ALWAYS BE IN YOUR LIFE, EVEN THOUGH THEY ARE NOT PRESENT.

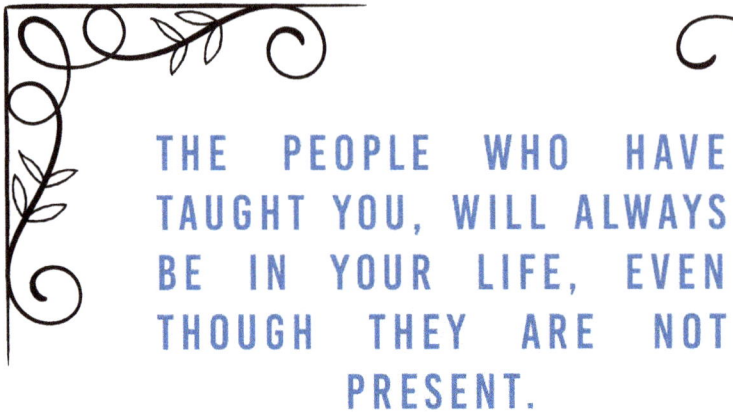

AS WE TRAVEL LIFE'S JOUR-
NEY, PEOPLE ARE PUT IN
OUR PATH TO CARRY US
ALONG UNTIL WE BECOME
WHO WE WERE MEANT TO
BECOME.

ABSENT FATHERS SHOULD BE THERE TO TAKE CARE OF THEIR CHILDREN AND VINDICTIVE MOTHERS SHOULD ALLOW FATHERS TO BE THERE.

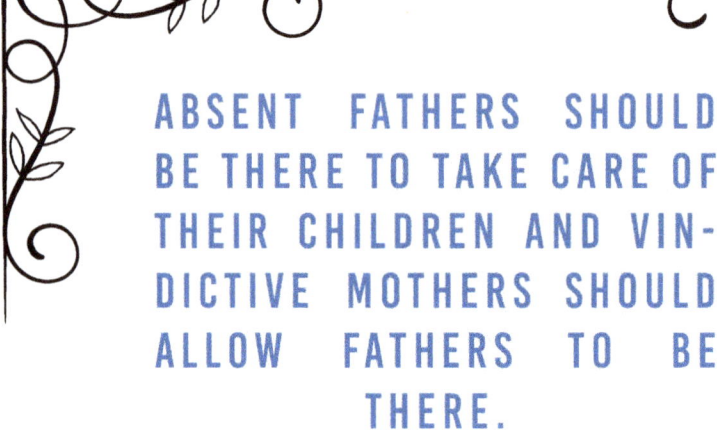

TEACH YOUNG BOYS AND GIRLS THE TRUE MEANING OF THE RITE OF PASSAGE EARLY ON AND THEY WILL CROSS THAT PASSAGE SUCCESSFULLY.

CRITICIZING THE POOR DOES NOT MAKE YOU A BETTER PERSON. IT SHOWS WHO YOU REALLY ARE.

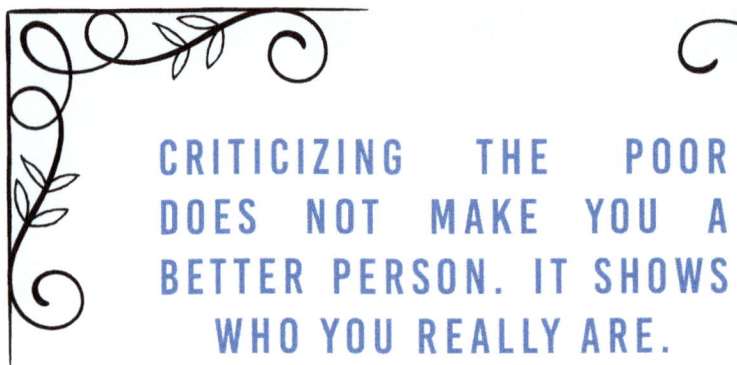

NO ONE SHOULD BE BORN
INTO A WORLD OF POVERTY
AND HAVE TO LIVE IN POV-
ERTY WHEN THERE IS SUCH
AN ABUNDANCE OF WEALTH
AND RICHES WORLDWIDE.

AS A PARENT, TAKE TIME TO LISTEN TO THE WORDS THAT COME OUT OF YOUR CHILD'S MOUTH. THEY MAY BE TRYING TO TELL YOU SOME-THING.

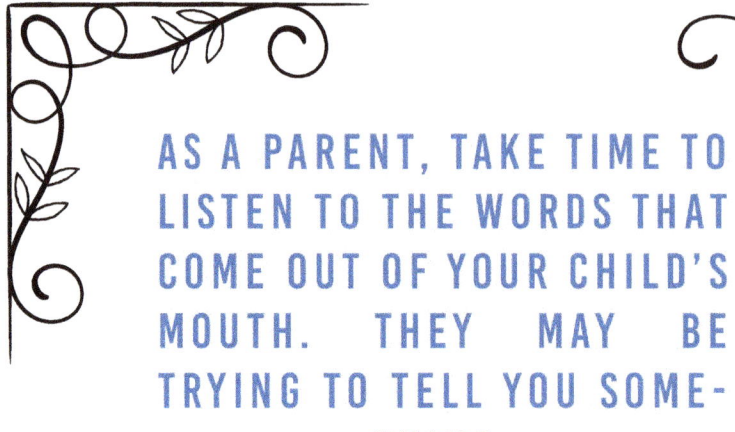

THE WAY YOU SEE LIFE IS THE WAY YOU THINK ABOUT LIFE.

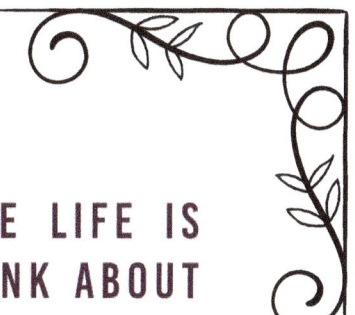

THEY SAY THAT THE YOUNG
WILL BECOME THE OLD BUT
WILL THE YOUNG EMBRACE
THE OLD?

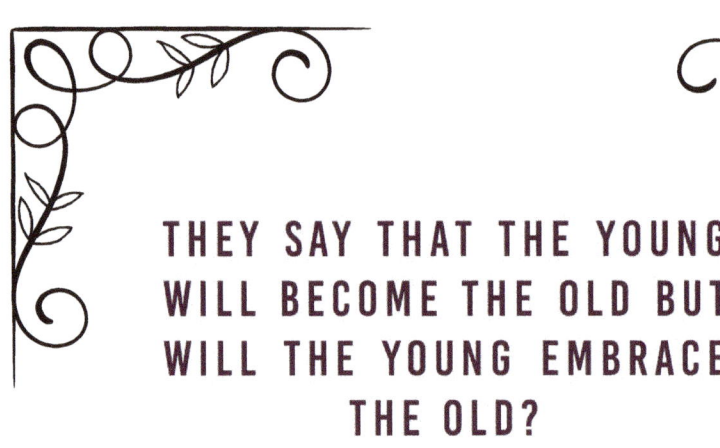

THE SUN RISES IN THE EAST AND SETS IN THE WEST. THIS WILL NEVER CHANGE. ACCEPT THE THINGS THAT WE CANNOT CHANGE.

DO NOT LOSE HOPE
BECAUSE IF YOU DO,
YOU'VE LOST THE RACE.

IF YOU STAY THE COURSE, PERSEVERE, AND HAVE AN ABIDING FAITH IN GOD, YOU WILL ACHIEVE GREAT THINGS.

SOMETIMES THE WORLD SEEMS LIKE IT IS SPINNING OUT OF CONTROL. COVID 19 ALLOWED THE SPINNING TO SLOW DOWN AND ALLOWED US TO PAUSE AND RESET.

THOSE WHO ARE INCARCER-
ATED SHOULD NOT BE FOR-
GOTTEN. ONE KIND WORD
OR ONE WORD OF ENCOUR-
AGEMENT MAY MAKE ALL
THE DIFFERENCE IN A LIFE
WELL LIVED.

ALWAYS TREAT EVERYONE WITH KINDNESS AND RESPECT AND IT WILL COME BACK TO YOU IN WAYS UNIMAGINABLE.

DURING THOSE TIMES OF GRIEF,
YOUR MERE PRESENCE MAY BE
A LOT MORE POWERFUL THAN
YOUR WORDS.

WHEN I WAS A LITTLE BOY, I REMEMBER WALKING BEHIND MY FATHER BECAUSE I COULD NOT KEEP UP. WHEN HE BECAME OLDER, HE WALKED BEHIND ME BECAUSE HE COULD NOT KEEP UP.

THINGS THAT SEEM UN-
REACHABLE ARE REACHABLE
AS LONG AS YOU STRETCH
YOUR IMAGINATION.